W9-BEV-700

My healthy body

Bobbie Kalman

 Crabtree Publishing Company

www.crabtreebooks.com

Created by Bobbie Kalman

Author and Editor-in-Chief
Bobbie Kalman

Educational consultants
Reagan Miller
Elaine Hurst
Joan King

Editors
Joan King
Reagan Miller
Kathy Middleton

Proofreader
Crystal Sikkens

Design
Bobbie Kalman
Katherine Berti

Photo research
Bobbie Kalman

Production coordinator
Katherine Berti

Prepress technician
Katherine Berti

Photographs
iStockphoto: p. 15 (top right)
Shutterstock: cover, p. 1, 3, 4, 5, 6, 7, 8, 9,
        10, 11, 12, 13, 14, 15 (except top right)

Library and Archives Canada Cataloguing in Publication

Kalman, Bobbie, 1947-
     My healthy body / Bobbie Kalman.

(My world)
ISBN 978-0-7787-9427-1 (bound).--ISBN 978-0-7787-9471-4 (pbk.)

     1. Children--Health and hygiene--Juvenile literature. 2. Health--
Juvenile literature. I. Title. II. Series: My world (St. Catharines, Ont.)

RA777.K34 2010   j613'.0432   C2009-906063-9

Library of Congress Cataloging-in-Publication Data

Kalman, Bobbie.
 My healthy body / Bobbie Kalman.
     p. cm. -- (My world)
 ISBN 978-0-7787-9471-4 (pbk. : alk. paper) -- ISBN 978-0-7787-9427-1
 (reinforced library binding : alk. paper)
 1. Children--Health and hygiene--Juvenile literature. 2. Health--Juvenile
 literature. I. Title.

 RA777.K35 2010
 613'.0432--dc22
                                         2009041179

Crabtree Publishing Company

www.crabtreebooks.com   1-800-387-7650

Printed in China/122009/CT20091009

Published in Canada
Crabtree Publishing
616 Welland Ave.
St. Catharines, Ontario
L2M 5V6

Published in the United States
Crabtree Publishing
PMB 59051
350 Fifth Avenue, 59th Floor
New York, New York 10118

Published in the United Kingdom
Crabtree Publishing
Maritime House
Basin Road North, Hove
BN41 1WR

Published in Australia
Crabtree Publishing
386 Mt. Alexander Rd.
Ascot Vale (Melbourne)
VIC 3032

Words to know

bath
(shower)

doctor
(dentist)

fruits

vegetables

sports
(soccer)

sunlight

water

I have a healthy body.
I can do many things.

I can run.

I can jump high.

My healthy body needs to be fit.
I bend and stretch in the morning.
I stay active all day long.

6

Playing **sports** keeps me fit, too.
I like to play **soccer**.
I run and kick the ball.

My healthy body needs clean air.
Trees clean the air I breathe.

My healthy body needs **sunlight**.
I get sunlight outside.

My healthy body needs **water**.
I drink plenty of water every day.

My healthy body needs good food.
I eat food that keeps me healthy.
Fruits and **vegetables** are great!

My healthy body needs to be clean.
I wash myself in a **bath** or **shower**.

I brush my teeth
after I eat.
I also brush
my tongue.
I floss my teeth
every day.

More ways to keep healthy

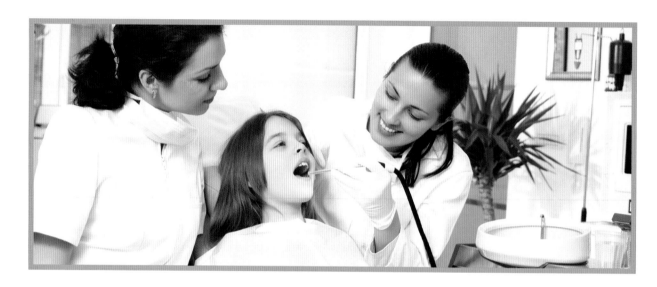

I visit the **dentist** twice a year.

My **doctor** helps
keep me healthy.
I visit her for checkups
and when I am sick.

I stay at home
when I am sick.

I sneeze
into my
arm.

I wash my hands
with soap.
I sing the
"Happy Birthday"
song while I wash.

I wash my hands
- before I eat
- after I go to
  the bathroom
- after I cough
  or sneeze
- after I touch
  an animal
- after I touch
  another
  person's hand

Notes for adults

Good health habits

My healthy body shows children the things that are necessary for good health—sunshine, clean air and water, nutritious food, and exercise. Children are close together at school and often get sick. With seasonal flu and H1N1, it can be hard to stay healthy. You can help them develop a plan for staying healthy by reviewing with them the essentials of health each day. They can eat a good breakfast every morning. At school, they can drink plenty of water and wash their hands often. Children could practice singing the "Happy Birthday" song as they wash their hands, to understand the importance of washing their hands with soap for a certain length of time.

Active kids contains easy-to-do physical activities for fitness and health.

Breakfast Blast contains healthy breakfast recipes and suggestions.

Exercise every day

Make a large exercise chart. Every day for a week, ask the children how they moved their bodies the day before—skipping, walking, running, playing hopscotch, dancing, or playing any sport such as soccer. You could also do some simple exercises with the children, as well as stretching or yoga.